God Provides Victory through Gideon

Judges 6:1–7:25

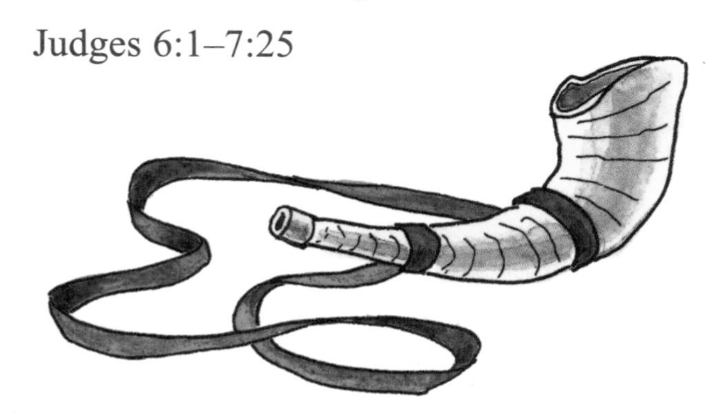

Written by Joanne Bader
Illustrated by Unada Gliewe

Arch® Books

3558 S. Jefferson Avenue, St. Louis, MO 63118-3968
Manufactured in the Colombia

God's people called the Israelites
Lived in a special place.
This land named Canaan was so great,
A gift from God through grace.

As time went by, the Israelites
Forgot God and His Word.
They worshiped idols made of stone;
Their love for Him had blurred.

It was not long before these folks
Had enemies galore
Who came from nearby Midian,
A land that was next door.

The Midianites were very mean.
They ate the people's food.
They stole their crops, camped on their land,
And acted very rude!

The Israelites were scared of them,
They crawled in caves to hide.
At last they prayed to God for help—
Asked Him to be their guide.

One day a man named Gideon,
Was threshing a field of wheat,
When suddenly an angel came
And sat down near his feet.

"Oh, Gideon," the angel said,
"You have a job to do.
You are a mighty warrior,
And God will strengthen you.

"The Israelites need lots of help,
And you must lead the fight.
Your men will beat the Midianites,
The Lord will be your might."

"But," he replied, "I am so weak!
Why has God chosen me?"
He asked God for some signs or proof,
Before he would agree.

When he was sure that God would help,
He said, "Yes, I'll obey."
He blew his trumpet, soldiers came,
Not all of them could stay.

And then God told him, “Send those home
Who say they are afraid.”
Though thousands left, too many stayed;
Their minds could not be swayed.

The Lord commanded, “Send more home!
Go to the river’s brink.
Choose men who lap the water up,
Not those who kneel to drink.”

Three hundred men and Gideon
Lined up around the camp.
Each had a trumpet, pitcher, torch.
How could they be the champ?

They blew their horns and smashed the jars.
Their torches burned so bright.
The enemy woke up and ran,
God's people won the fight!

As God had promised Gideon
He'd helped in every way.
The army did not fight alone,
God fought with them that day.

You, too, are His chosen child.
This story is for you!
Commit your way unto the Lord;
Trust Him in all you do.

Dear Parents,

When children hear amazing stories like this one, they might think of Gideon as a superhero. However, it is important for them to realize that Gideon won a great victory for the Lord and with His guidance that day. Gideon was not a great man, but God chose him to do an important job. Gideon thought he was weak and doubted his ability to do it. The Lord helped Gideon do the job, just as He promised He would.

All of us have been chosen by God. He has a plan for our lives; He is always with us and will provide all that we need. We do not have to be afraid. In Deuteronomy 31:6, we are told, "Be strong and courageous. Do not be afraid or terrified because of them, for the Lord your God goes with you; He will never leave you nor forsake you."

The greatest thing you can do is remind your children of God's commitment to them through Holy Baptism. Because of what God has done, we can do the things He has planned for us.

The Author